FREEMASONRY

A PROGRESSIVE
SCIENCE

R. W. Hudson

First published 2020
Copyright © 2020 R.W.Hudson

British Library Cataloguing in Publication Data

A catalogue record for this book is available from the British Library

ISBN-13: 978-1-913751-00-5

Cover Illustration:

Masonic Square and Compasses
above the motto: 'Faith, Hope and Charity'.

CONTENTS

INTRODUCTION

Among Non-Masons, especially the sensationalist type, and even among many Freemasons, there are many misconceptions, misunderstandings, of the original objectives of Freemasonry, so much so that much of the original true meanings and objectives of Freemasonic ritual have become blurred and confused.

It seems very much to me that the original creators of this system of character building, social understanding, harmonising with your fellow man, and creating a better understanding of the individuals relationship with whatever he deems his God to be, which eventually evolved into our Freemasonry as practised today, were very intelligent individuals with a serious intent regarding the most suitable method of encouraging others in how to achieve what they felt was the best way to reach such high objectives. By this system of progression of serious, but most enjoyable, enactments based upon either biblical or events in recognised history, it was hoped that man's understanding of himself and his God would lead eventually to peaceful harmony throughout life.

So great was its objectives and construction that, like most things in life, it received many imitators, some not quite understanding and therefore not achieving the ideals set by the original creators. But others, managing to take the original objectives a little further, hence we have many Freemasonic Orders within our system, thereby confirming the dictate that Freemasonry is a progressive science.

In my attempt to "get back to basics" I trust that I have brought some light upon what is, without doubt, in my humble opinion, the greatest method of self-improvement, ever devised by man. In saying this I give full respect to the many spiritual and mystical systems that are abundant in many cultures, but they appear to me to be specific for those so inclined, whereas Freemasonry appeals and satisfies on many levels. Freemasonry is "free" from any dogma that has a tendency to confine and thereby limit thought and development. Its members are free to interpret as they see and feel and are able to participate and express their thoughts and feelings, unlike the established church which restricts active participation to a small group, called the congregation, with the main work being conducted by specially trained operatives that are obliged to stay within established teachings. Limitation frustrates development and progress.

How did Freemasonry come into being?, is a question that has attracted many academics as well as speculative answers that become so obtuse and complicated that to be able to draw some comfort in the form of a sensible conclusion is virtually impossible. So for myself I have my own conclusion that is simple and logical, as in reality, most things are. Having ignored the majority of the speculative theses I now present my own.

Freemasonry, like many similar systems in life is no more than a belief system, it is a belief rather than a religious system'. It attempts to encourage you to find answers for yourself regarding the major important aspects of life. Your relationship with whatever your God may be, your relationship within your community, your respect and support for your sovereign, country and neighbour, but perhaps more importantly your relationship with yourself and nature.

Since time immemorial man has always wanted to know how things came into being. Where did our Earth come from, where did we come from, who made everything. Each culture, since the beginning, has formulated its own view based on its knowledge of things at that time. This original view changes as knowledge becomes available and greater understanding arrives from such developing knowledge. Also the infiltration of knowledge that, with travel, becomes grafted on to existing beliefs and so modifies through the conduit of Magi, Priests, Mystics, the Church and eventually Science over time. So logically, if we simply start with the Sumerians who, in the innocence of their lack of actual knowledge, formulated their theories based on what they knew at that time, and then it became known by another culture that took their theories to a large extent and added their understanding, which then in turn became the basis for another culture to take and adjust to suit their attitudes, coming all the way through to the Arab nations and other peoples of the Middle East with the conduit being what we now call Religion. "Hence we have three of the world's main religions, Judaism, Christianity and Islam, all based around the same origin theories with slight adjustments and understandings of the same basic facts. They are all Abrahamic belief systems or what is known collectively as "Peoples of the Book."

For an excellent illustration of such changes and adaptations we only have to look at two of the most powerful and influential cultures, The Greeks and the Romans. Both these cultures originally had a myriad of Gods within their own belief system. Then gradually, over time, both cultures came to adopt a particular developing belief system that became known as Christianity. A close look at each of these belief systems will discover many similarities that have been taken from each other and grafted on to the newly adopted system, that tended to make it perhaps more acceptable to the peoples of each culture, as a few aspects of their original religion were woven into the newly accepted one.

Although the same basics exist in each for their own belief system, these three religions are fiercely defended, and in some cases, fiercely attacked, at times, by each other, even though they contain the same principals and code of moral conduct, and this has continued over the millennia.

It has to be acknowledged that over the millennia the Jewish belief system has encouraged learning and education as a prime motivation to finding answers for the constant question of origins etc. Whilst other belief systems have developed in similar ways, the Jewish faith has concentrated more heavily on knowledge and education and slightly less on dogma etc.   We must remember that the Knights Templar sojourned for at least 200 years in this part of the world and would have been exposed to all the contents of these varying belief systems. Catholicism was not only the backers of the Knights Templar, but was at the same time the most powerful and strongest faith in the then known world. To entertain differing views, no matter how obtained would have been regarded as heresy, and the appropriate action taken. History itself records those actions and atrocities conducted by the Roman Catholic faith in order to maintain its supposed supremacy. The Knights Templar not only learned from the various belief systems within the Middle East, but also gained actual knowledge to support differing interpretations and understandings of their Roman Catholic Faith. In order not to suffer the tortures etc., of exposing their knowledgeable gains they kept things secret and practised them in private away from prying eyes and ears.

Freemasonry today, and possibly for the last couple of centuries, claims its origin from the Guilds and the ancient Stone masons. I have explained in detail in my earlier books that this simply cannot be true and is also illogical, and I detail all the reasons in my former books. On the other hand there are many, many reasons within Freemasonic ritual itself to claim the Knights Templar as a source for its traditions, principles and tenets. The heavy stress on the stonemason's art can be simply explained in that the Knights Templar had a building arm, just like they had a fighting arm, a "banking" arm, and a maritime arm. This building arm has been proved to be responsible for many great churches, cathedrals, and castles that abound throughout Europe. Finally, this building arm was known as "The Children Of Solomon." When the Knights Templar endured the persecutions of Philip le Bel and the Pope back in 1307 plus, the Children of Solomon were exempt from the heresy charges and allowed to go free. It is not illogical to suppose that some important Knights slipped into this absolved group in order for them to preserve their principles, tenets and beliefs. The power of the Church continued for many centuries but gradually decreased as some sovereigns, governments, and individuals became stronger and therefore bolder and began to challenge the formerly accepted religious authority. Finally, possibly with the Age of Enlightenment, the Templars belief system, now greatly modified over the centuries with new archaeological evidence and understanding, could now quietly reveal itself in its new guise as FREEMASONRY. I have in my previous book given many historical connections and events plus a great many clues within modern day Masonic ritual that support my concluded theory.

Part of the teaching within Freemasonry is that it has existed, in some form or other, from "TIME IMMEMORIAL", which can be taken to mean "from the beginning of time itself". Whereas the operative craft of building with stone has existed naturally only from the stone age, and whereas the various prehistoric belief systems have been in existence since man first became into being, I trust the logic of my conclusion can be appreciated.

Having fully explained the Craft in "SO YOU THINK YOU KNOW ABOUT FREEMASONRY" and the Holy Royal Arch in "SO YOU THINK YOU KNOW ABOUT THE CHAPTER", I can now attempt to illustrate many of the other Masonic Orders or "Side Degrees" as they have now become known.

For those new Freemasons and Non-Freemasons who may be reading this book, I will explain the difference between an Order and a Degree.

A degree within Freemasonry is a ceremony containing a sign, a token which is some physical proof of authenticity usually some handshake or other manual gesticulation, and a secret word. An Order is a collection of degrees that illustrate a progression through the story being illustrated. So anyone who says they know the Masonic Handshake should be able to demonstrate many scores of such varying handshakes. In the Craft alone there are at least 7 different handshakes through the 4 degrees.

Ray Hudson
February 2017

CHAPTER 1
MARK MASTER MASON

The qualification required for advancement to this degree is that you must be a Master Mason under the United Grand Lodge of England.

The Mark Degree is part of what is known as "The Solomonic Degrees", and is an important and informative part of the continuing story of the building of King Solomon's Temple.

The Order of Mark Master Mason takes its provenance from the second degree of the Craft, as in the olden times there were only two degrees in Craft Freemasonry namely Entered Apprentice and Fellowcraft. There was no Master Mason degree until much later, which is why the Master Elect of a Craft Lodge takes his initial Obligation within the second or Fellowcraft degree and not as one might expect from the 3rd degree or Master Mason's degree as it is known.

The Mark degree is much older than the Craft 3rd degree and there is supportive evidence in Scotland that a form of the Mark degree ceremony was conducted as early as 1599, over 2 centuries before the coming together of the Ancients and Moderns.

It is quoted in Mackey's Revised Encyclopedia of Freemasonry:

"The antiquity of Mark Masonry cannot be doubted. Operatively considered and even speculatively, it has enjoyed special prominence for centuries. Brethren, according to existing records, dating back to 1600, in which year, on June 8, "Ye principal warden and Chief master of maisons, Wm. Schaw, master of work to ye Kingis Maistie, met members of the Lodge of Edinburgh – now No. 1 – at Holyrood House, at which meeting the Laird of Auchinleck was present, and attested the minutes of the assembly by his Mark, as did the Operatives in accordance with the Schaw Statutes of December 28, 1598, which provided: "That the day of reassauying, or receiving, of said fellow of craft or master be ord'lie buikit and his name and Mark insert in the said buik"

For me there is a great deal of confusion regarding the statement issued at the time when the Ancients and Moderns had their coming together between 1813 and 1815, when they declared, "Pure and Ancient Freemasonry consists only of 3 Degrees, Entered Apprentice, Fellow Craft and Master Mason, including that of the Holy Royal Arch". Many believe that this statement completely excludes not only the very important Mark Degree but also all the other equally important Masonic Orders. I have a simple and logical explanation for this confusion and mis-understanding. The Moderns called their ritual *"PURE"*, whilst the Ancients, naturally referred to their ritual as being *"ANCIENT"*. So they are simply referring to that work which they particularly conduct and supervise. There is no direct reference to any other Masonic Order. They could just have easily said "Ancient and Modern Freemasonry consist only of......." Or even better having formed the United Grand Lodge of England, that "United Grand Lodge of England Freemasonry consists only of......". Which is perfectly true and unambiguous. Quite recently we have had our Grand Master the Duke of Kent together with Prince Michael of Kent announce an acknowledgement to the connectivity and importance of all the Masonic Orders. How true this acknowledgement is, and also how important an acknowledgment of this magnitude is to the whole beautiful Masonic system. The essential added knowledge that is portrayed within the ceremonials of the so called, side orders or high degrees, adds so much to the overall knowledge of the Masonic teachings that their importance cannot be overstated. It was not until 1856 that the Mark Grand Lodge was independently formed, and from that formation the Mark Degree has ever grown and continues to add lustre and knowledge to the 3 principal Craft Degrees, and I might add that the Mark Degree does add to greater understanding of some other Masonic Orders that I will be covering within this book.

There is evidence within the Craft Lodge furniture of the Mark Degree's existence in England prior to the 3rd Craft degree which can be found on the 3rd Degree Tracing Board within most Craft Lodges. On the 3rd Degree Tracing Board, among other things, there is a secret code that can only be explained by use of the key used in the Mark Degree ceremony. Once decoded there is a message for every Master Mason but rarely, unfortunately, is it ever explained. I have known Freemasons of 5o year's masonic experience that have never had that code explained to them, therefore that secret message is lost to them, and not knowing of its existence, they have never enquired about it. When I have explained it in detail at a Craft Lodge to the assembled Master Masons and above, the surprise on their faces is quite incredible. If you have read my earlier book "So you think you know about Freemasonry" in which I explain the significance of this code and detail the interpretation of the relevant symbols contained on the Craft 3rd degree Tracing Board, you will have seen the full explanation and now understand the senior age of the Mark Master Mason's degree.

Another clue to the positive connectivity of the Mark Degree to the Craft hovers around the individual named Adoniram. Dr. Mackey's Encyclopaedia of Freemasonry quotes that Hiram Abiff was married to Adoniram's sister, meaning that both men were brothers-in-law. When you appreciate and understand the close working family relationship that existed, and in fact still exists, within the Jewish culture, the close relationship of these two characters so detailed throughout many Masonic Orders becomes a lot more positive, lending a greater possibility of credibility that takes our thoughts beyond legend and myth. An interesting fact that endorses my comments regarding these two individuals is that the name of the person within the Masonic legend that occupies the chair within a Craft lodge is Adoniram. So many Freemasons when asked the question "who is that who occupies the chair in a Craft Lodge?" reply "King Solomon". This cannot be so as the person in the chair is ".....the humble representative of King Solomon" and therefore cannot be King Solomon himself. Yes, it is the Chair of King Solomon, but it is not King Solomon who occupies it. It is the individual who is beckoned three times by King Solomon as enacted within the Installation degree of a Craft Lodge. It is the individual who attempts to bow before King Solomon but is prevented from performing such an obeisant gesture to the King, and is then placed in the chair of Solomon by the King himself. That individual is Adoniram, so it is him who is the humble representative of King Solomon. From this action we can now fully appreciate the close connection of the Mark Master Mason's degree to that of the Fellow Craft, as Adoniram is a very important person or word within the Mark Master Mason's degree. Furthermore the word of an Installed Master of the Craft describes a particular type of craftsman within the trade of building, which Solomon, by his royal status, certainly was not, but Adoniram certainly was. This proves the name of the person that occupies the chair of King Solomon and is therefore the humble representative of that royal personage..

In Scotland the Mark Degree does form a natural part of the Craft and Chapter ceremonies of a Masonic Lodge. This I know as I belong to Canongate & Kilwinning Chapter No. 56. In Edinburgh and attend their meetings at least once a year.

The Mark degree does prove extremely popular among Freemasons as the ceremony, although containing serious principles and tenets, also adding much to the understanding of the building of King Solomon's Temple, does lend itself to a relaxed, and at times, amusing interpretation of parts of the ritual. This always makes the Candidate feel relaxed and is certainly an important part of what is actually happening within the ceremony.

I have stated that the Mark Degree follows on from the 2nd Degree of the Craft – The Fellow Craft- and therefore relates to a period just before the death of Hiram Abiff. It is a very instructive degree and teaches the lesson that education is the reward of labour.

From its very title Mark Master Mason one can derive that it contains much information about the Marks of the Stonemasons throughout the distant past. These Marks can be found on various parts of many old churches, castles etc. etc. They were effected for especial reasons. First so that the Overseer could establish who actually prepared the stone, second the Mark also told of the exact position of the stone within the structure and of its relationship to the abutting stone. The stone masons of old could not write as such, so created their Marks to establish their identity. This system is enacted within the ceremony and you keep your Mark throughout your career within the Mark Degree. In fact your "Mark" can be inscribed on the Jewel that you are invested with at the appropriate part of the Advancement ceremony.

The governing body of the Mark Degree or Mark Grand Lodge was formed in 1856 and currently has its headquarters at Mark Mason's Hall at 86, St. James's Street, London SW1A 1PL. This address is also the headquarters for most of the other Masonic Orders that form the greater part of this Progressive Science. The governing body of Mark Master Masons justifiably prides itself on its great charitable work for which it is famous. The extensive work that it does in this direction is widely acknowledged for its speedy response and effectiveness in distributing funds wherever needed and whenever found to be required within the Masonic system and within the non-masonic world wherever the need is greatest. The ardent Mark Master Mason is always proud to be a part of this duly acknowledged great charitable work and the professional manner in which it is administered. A tremendous product of this wonderful degree.

Having given some background and history of the Mark Degree, we will now look at the ceremony itself. Again I will not be revealing any secrets but hope to give some insight into what is an extremely instructive, informative and very happy degree.

The Mark Master Masons Degree is called an Advancement, and it is a natural advancement in the instruction of the building of a particular part of the Holy Temple. It is also a re-enactment of the importance of that part of the Craft 2nd Degree Tracing Board Lecture that describes the Fellows of the Craft obtaining and receiving their wages. Within the ceremony you see each stone that has been cut, squared and marked presented to 3 Overseers or, in modern terms, Foremen or Inspectors who meticulously examine each stone for smoothness, exact size and that it is free of cracks or any other such fault that would render it unfit, and that it is in exact accordance with the plans that they have for the inspection.

Suddenly a stone of a different size and shape is presented to the 1st Overseer, and after some ad-lib discussion between the "guide" and the Candidate, which, being ad-lib, can lead to some quite humorous exchanges, there is then a progression on to another Overseer which is similar to that of the 1st, with similar adlib exchanges. Finally we have arrival at the "Gaffer" or Master Overseer who is less tolerant of this rogue stone that does not match up to his plans, and after registering his annoyance causes it to be thrown amongst all the other rejected stones.

Then there is panic as the Chair enquires where the special stone is and gives strict instructions for the search to be made, and to bring it to him when found together with the Fellowcraft who made it. This is done and the reward is that he is made a Mark Master Mason, with full ceremonial and explanation of the principles and moral lessons derived from the enactment of the ceremony.

The prose and principles of this degree are really something to be heard and absorbed, as the ceremony is structured to be fully enjoyed. The usual passwords, signs, grips and secret words are similarly contained in this degree and are imparted within the conferral of the degree in the usual Masonic style.

This is a fascinating and worthwhile degree, and throws much light on many aspects of the Solomonic Degrees of Freemasonry which explore aspects of King Solomon's Temple, so much so that it is a requirement that this degree be obtained before progression can be effected into certain other Masonic Orders within this progressive science.

As the Mark Master Masons Degree follows on from the 2nd Degree of the Craft, it would make perfect sense if an aspiring Craft Mason elected to have this Advancement before entering the Holy Royal Arch. Historically and chronologically that decision would make perfect sense.

Attached to many of the other Masonic Orders is what might be termed an "Appendant Order", that is either a degree that has some connection to the main Order or one that could be conferred as a degree of merit on a deserving Freemason. The Mark degree has a degree attached to it that it is not conferred as a degree of honour but is another option that the decision to join is entirely up to the individual.

That degree is called:

CHAPTER 2
THE ANCIENT AND HONOURABLE
FRATERNITY OF ROYAL ARK MARINERS.

This degree celebrates the story of Noah, his sons, the Great Flood, and, of course, the Ark or Noah's Ark. The story is lifted directly from Genesis of the Old Testament and details the events portrayed therein of the idolatry of the people, the piety of Noah, the building of the Ark and the covenant between Noah and his God.

The connection between this Royal Ark Mariner degree and the Mark Degree is somewhat obtuse and is little appreciated by many, many Freemasons.

Noah had 3 sons, namely Shem, Japheth and Ham. Ham was a very naughty son and was subsequently banished by Noah and his family to some far off land. In true biblical fashion there was a replacement of Ham in the form of an individual named Adoniram. Although in those biblical times individuals are quoted as having lived hundreds of years as did Methuselah, I cannot believe that this Adoniram was the same person as that portrayed in the Mark degree. Chronologically the gap is too far distant. This was quite a common name in those far off biblical times. But it does give a connection, tenuous as it may be. We must not forget that according to the bible, Noah was apparently 500 years old when his first child was born. It seems logical that mention of these extreme longevities are purely an indication of a period of time and perhaps not indicative of the true length of time.

As the events depicted in this degree take place long before Moses and therefore long before the writings of the Old Testament there is no Volume of the Sacred Law present. A particular object, identical to the one much used by Noah is present and represents a sacred aspect on which to make the solemn promises inculcated in this degree.

The story of the falling from grace of the people, the subsequent wrath of their God and His relationship with Noah and his family are portrayed in much detail. Noah is instructed to build an Ark that will preserve him and his family from the impending deluge. The biblical story is followed quite closely. The candidate is "Elevated" to this degree and the pious life and principles of Noah are exemplified in wonderful detail and prose. His building of the Ark and the sending out first of the Raven, and then the Dove are highlighted in the signs and secrets of the Degree.

In the 3 Craft degrees there are certain steps that are emphasised namely in the Entered Apprentice Degree three steps are taken, in the Fellow Craft degree 5 steps are taken and in the Master Masons Degree 7 steps are taken. In this degree 9 steps are taken and there is a wonderful explanation of these nine steps given at the appropriate time in the ceremony. But, as has often happened with various rituals within Freemasonry, the governing body change it, they hope for the better understanding within modern times, but on this occasion of the wonderful explanation of the nine steps, they appear to have made a gigantic error. There are no particular secrets within the explanation of the nine steps, simply a wonderful description and explanation of the various excellent attributes that are attached and exemplified to each of the nine steps within this lovely degree. The attributes, originally, were WISDOM, STRENGTH, BEAUTY, CONTEMPLATION, WATCHFULNESS,

DISCRETION, BROTHERLY LOVE, TRUTH, CHARITY. For some reason that I am totally unaware of, the attribute of CONTEMPLATION was removed from the ritual in 1985 by the guardians of our ceremonies within Mark Masons Hall. The manner in which this part of the ceremony is delivered is such a wonderful and important part of the Elevation ceremony that to omit the most important part of this explanation reduces its beauty and therefore the total meaning of the whole explanation is somewhat damaged. There are still nine steps, but only eight attributes are mentioned with their importance and necessity described. This omission of the fourth attribute holds no logic or reason, but hopefully in time the guardians may see sense and restore it to its former glory and total understanding. That's enough from my soapbox, now to continue.

The story of the deluge, Noah, the Ark and the final covenant bestowed by God is further exemplified with all the traditional "extras" that any regular Masonic ceremony contains. The virtues demonstrated by Noah, and the necessity for avoiding the idolatrous ways pursued by the people are soundly exemplified and the virtues encouraged whilst the idolatrous lifestyle is summarily discouraged. All demonstrated in an excellent style that is greatly enjoyable and is totally worthwhile.

This degree not only portrays the biblical narrative in a much more plausible manner but emphasises the piety and behavioural principles of Noah in a more modern attitude that if respected can only improve ones self and ultimately reflect on those nearest and dearest to him.

CHAPTER 3

UNITED RELIGIOUS, MILITARY & MASONIC ORDERS OF THE TEMPLE AND OF ST. JOHN OF JERUSALEM, PALESTINE, RHODES & MALTA, IN ENGLAND AND WALES & PROVINCES OVERSEAS.

This military chivalric Order has attached to it great historic qualities and much romantic attraction. The Knights Templar have been shrouded in mystery and speculation ever since their inception around 1100 AD. Many books and articles have been written about this original Order of warrior monks, some of it pure romance but much of it being based upon solid research and careful study. It is even speculated by many academics that the Knights Templar are the most likely source for the origins of what is our Freemasonry today.

The qualification for joining this Order is that you must be a Master Mason and also a member of the Holy Royal Arch, or Chapter, as it is more popularly known. And as the original Knights Templar were a Christian Knightly Order backed by the Holy Roman Catholic Church the Candidate must subscribe to the Christian Trinitarian Faith, meaning to have a solid belief in the Father, Son and Holy Ghost. Those criteria being established application can be justly effected.

Once accepted, the regalia required is completed with an Alb, Mantle, Cap, Belt, Frog and sword plus Jewels.

The Candidate is first prepared as a Pilgrim requiring refreshment and rest within a Knights Templar Preceptory and expresses a desire to be admitted a member. Within some Knights Templar Preceptories a VIGIL used to be conducted, but this is not now the case. The Candidate undergoes a pilgrimage and then a symbolic warfare. Also he must serve a year (symbolically) of Penance. Certain aspects of the history of the Order are related, and the usual Masonic obligations conducted. He is then knighted and regaled in the garb of a Knights Templar.

The whole ceremony is conducted naturally in a very militaristic manner and the atmosphere is one of great appeal not only to the Candidate but also to the assembled Knights.

This Masonic Order has great appeal for many Freemasons and the ceremonies justly merit its popularity and appeal. The military style, sword drill, history and romance that has become traditional to the Knights Templar, plus within man there appears to be an innate desire to "team-up" and form a military unit, especially one that has the history and the mystery the Knights Templar have acquired. All these factors make for a wonderful Order and involvement that fully justifies its popularity and purpose.

There is also attached to this Order the Appendant Order of the Knights of Malta or the Knights Hospitaller.

CHAPTER 4
THE ANCIENT AND MASONIC ORDER OF ST. JOHN OF JERUSALEM, PALESTINE, RHODES & MALTA.

These were originally formed to give aid and succour to the pilgrims who travelled to the Holy Land at the time of the crusades.

Many academics believe that the real origin of the Knights stems from the ancient Merchants of Amalfi started about 600AD by a group of Jewish merchants who took care of the sick and aided the poor. As time progressed and life changed so that about the year 1000AD a group of crusader knights joined them to assist their safety and so you have the attachment to the Knights Templar, although this is not factually proved in history.

This modern degree is similarly Christian as the Knights Templar and requires a like affinity to the Trinitarian Faith. The work and travels of these knights is commemorated within the ceremonies. It has its own regalia but this is not insisted upon. The Knights Templar regalia can be continued to be worn.

Both the Knights Templar and the Knights of Malta are chivalric orders and exemplify the standards of chivalry aspired to in those olden times, but applies them in a modern context. Together with the military aspect and the marvellous ceremonies, both these Orders hold a fascinating interest for many Freemasons.

CHAPTER 5
ANCIENT AND ACCEPTED RITE FOR ENGLAND
& WALES, AND ITS DISTRICTS & PROVINCES
OVERSEAS

The qualification for joining this Christian Order is that you must be a Master Mason for 1 year under the UGLE and profess a belief in the Christian Trinitarian Faith.

As the title "Rose Croix" might imply the order is originally French being established around 1800 and is formally part of the "Ancient and Accepted Rite".

It is a system of 33 degrees, but the majority are rarely worked. The 3 Craft degrees constitute the first 3 Degrees of this order and the 4th to the 17th are conferred by rote.

The 18th degree, (the actual "Rose Croix" degree) is conducted as an entry into the Order, and it is during this ceremony that the 4th to the 17th Intermediate degrees are conferred. The 18th degree is called a degree of Perfection and one could say that it is an apt title. The ceremony is conducted in 3 different areas meant for Reflection, Searching and finally into the Light. Each part having an excellence that portrays precisely the mood required for each attribute. The final entry into the Light is quite spectacular and is meant to impress on each Perfectee's mind the importance of the message and lessons being demonstrated.

For any Christian Freemason this is a wonderful Order that will enhance and perhaps clarify his Christian beliefs and marry them to his Masonic principles with Faith, Hope and Charity.

CHAPTER 6

THE MASONIC AND MILITARY ORDER OF THE RED CROSS OF CONSTANTINE AND THE ORDERS OF THE HOLY SEPULCHRE AND OF ST. JOHN THE EVANGELIST.

To qualify to join this Order you must be a Master Mason and a member of the Holy Royal Arch, and also hold a belief in the Holy Christian Faith.

As the title illustrates this Order is made up of 3 degrees namely (1) Knight of the Red Cross of Constantine, (2) the Eminent Viceroy representing the Venerable Eusebius, (3) the Puissant Sovereign representing Constantine. It also has attached to it 2 Appendant Orders namely, (1) Knight of the Holy Sepulchre, (2) Knight of St. John the Evangelist. These 2 Appendant Orders are both single degrees.

This Order together with the 2 Appendant Orders exemplifies with full impact the history of Christianity as it became the Religion of Rome and of the lands that were under Roman authority.

The main character, The Emperor Constantine the Great, was a truly enigmatic character as history plainly illustrates. He was a great man of his time. A formidable warrior and leader of his armies, a political opportunist and very clever strategist. All these qualities when activated justly earned him the title "Great".

The degree of Knight of the Red Cross of Constantine is held in a Conclave and the Candidate enters as a Pilgrim in search of Divine knowledge. Promising to follow the example of the process of conversion to Christianity by Constantine and his making of it as the Religion of the whole of the Roman Empire when it was united by Constantine. The wonderful example of Constantine, and his actions towards the Christian slaves and the poor, is encouraged to be emulated in a modern context by the Candidate.

Once the Candidate has completed his Installation and is knighted, some extremely interesting historical information is given which reveals the importance of this Order to the Christian Faith and to the history of those times.

The first Appendant Order, that of The Order of the Holy Sepulchre is held in a Sanctuary, and refers to the discovery of the true cross by St. Helena, the mother of Constantine, and concerns the new knight grasping the significance of Jesus's life. Candidates are usually done "en bloc" within the Division together with the second Appendant Order Knight of St. John the Evangelist which concerns the ruins of the Temple at Jerusalem and the formation of the Knights of St. John and is conducted in a Commandery. They both have a tremendous impact adding much to the Order in general as well as adding much to the knights knowledge of his Christian Faith. Within these 2 Appendant Orders there is no progression, and consequently there is no chair. Although once proficient within the Order in general you can be invited to assist by participating in the conferral of these excellent Christian degrees on future candidates.

Again it is a Chivalric Military Order and contains and expresses all the usual attributes associated with Chivalric Masonic Knighthood, as well as gaining knowledge that assists in adding much more understanding for your appreciation of Christianity.

CHAPTER 7
THE ORDER OF ROYAL AND SELECT MASTERS
OF ENGLAND & WALES AND ITS DISTRICTS
AND COUNCILS OVERSEAS

This is possibly the most fascinating and interesting Masonic Order and to be eligible to join you must be a Master Mason, a companion of the Holy Royal Arch and a Mark Master Mason. The Order consists of 5 degrees; Select Master, Royal Master, Most Excellent Master and Super Excellent Master, the 5th Degree is the Installation ceremony which places the aspirant into the Chair and this degree also contains the usual Masonic secrets.

It also has attached to it 2 extra degrees, one is a degree of honour and is conferred according to merit and ability. It is entitled The Order of the Silver Trowel. The story enacted within the Silver Trowel ceremony is about the death of King David and the serious advice that is passed on by King David to his son Solomon.

The other is at the discretion of the District Grand Master obtaining the Grand Masters permission to confer the degree which is the equivalent of taking "The passing of the veils".

This Order explores the unique relationship between Hiram Abiff and Adoniram and in the Royal Master degree there is without doubt the finest portion of Masonic prose anywhere within the Masonic system of ceremonies.

Furthermore much knowledge is added to the Holy Royal Arch by the Most Excellent Master and the Super Excellent Master. The Select Master is the degree of admission into the Order.

It does fill in the gap between a Mark Master Mason Degree, which describes the preparation of the material for the building of the Temple, and the recovery of the word in the Holy Royal Arch.

This Order of the Royal and Select Masters really is an Order that offers much knowledge and understanding. And further assists in culminating the knowledge that any interested Freemason may have gained from the Craft and the Holy Royal Arch. A stronger recommendation to a participation in this Order cannot possibly be advised or recommended.

CHAPTER 8
THE ORDER OF THE ALLIED MASONIC DEGREES.

The qualification to join this Order is that you must be a Master Mason, a Companion of the Holy Royal Arch and a Mark Master Mason.

This Order contains 5 degrees, and although not directly linked to a single theme, offers much in extra knowledge to other Orders. The five degrees are:

1) The Order of St. Lawrence the Martyr.

2) The Knights of Constantinople.

3) The Grand Tilers of Solomon.

4) The Red cross of Babylon.

5) The Order of the Grand High Priest.

The first degree of St. Lawrence the Martyr commemorates the martyrdom of the Saint in Rome in about the middle of the 3rd Century A.D.

This is a very interesting degree that teaches the important qualities of fortitude and humility. It uses the martyrdom of St. Lawrence by the Roman Prefect of the time to exemplify the gracious qualities and ingenuity of St. Lawrence and encourages you to emulate the said qualities. The Temple is set up basically as a Craft Lodge with minor differences, but with the same Officers as a Craft Lodge.

The next degree is of The Knights of Constantinople which teaches the qualities of humility and universal equality. The Temple is once again set up basically as a Craft Lodge with some minor adjustments. This degree is about bringing the false superiority of the noble classes to the same level as the regarded common people, thereby demonstrating humility and equality.

The 3rd degree is The Grand Tilers of Solomon and warns of the dangers of carelessness and hasty judgement and teaches the importance of careful Tiling of the Lodge.

Having built a secret chamber beneath King Solomon's Temple, the three Grand Masters who bore sway over the building of the Temple, are sitting in this secret chamber discussing future plans when an intruder stumbles into their secret meeting because the chamber was not tiled properly. Thus are the necessities for proper Tiling and the need for attention to be careful and to refrain from hasty judgement, are amply exemplified.

The 4th Degree is that of The Red Cross of Babylon and exemplifies friendship and trust. It enacts the relationship between Zerubbabel and King Cyrus the Great, as mentioned slightly in the Holy Royal Arch, and the granting of the exiled Jews to return from their captivity in Babylon to Jerusalem and rebuild the second Temple.

This degree adds much to the degree of the Holy Royal Arch.

The 5th and final degree in this Order is The Holy Order of Grand High Priest. This degree, again, is closely associated with the Holy Royal Arch and deals with Abram's relationship with the Jewish High Priest Melchizedek. Abram's battles with the five Kings of the surrounding areas. This degree has a great history around the world under various constitutions at various times. It has the potential to make members appreciate a higher level of Masonic thought. It exemplifies to the Candidate that he is specifically chosen for some very important and high responsibilities, not only as a Freemason but also as a man.

These 5 Degrees add much knowledge to other earlier Orders and to the progressive nature of the man himself in his community life. Once admitted into the degree of St. Lawrence the Martyr, the other degrees can be taken in any other Allied Council which proves convenient.

CHAPTER 9
THE ORDER OF THE SECRET MONITOR OR BROTHERHOOD OF DAVID AND JONATHAN IN THE BRITISH ISLES AND ITS DISTRICTS AND CONCLAVES OVERSEAS.

The qualification for joining this order is simply that you must be a Master Mason.

The Order of the Secret Monitor or OSM, as it is more familiarly known is about the friendship and Brotherly Love between David and Jonathan as depicted in the Bible stories. The term Brotherly Love is mentioned and meant in the true Masonic sense of total regard and respect for each other, and should not be implied in any other sense. Jonathan is David's great friend and ally, and monitors his safety and well being in a secretive manner hence the phrase "Secret Monitor".

So important is the element of Brotherly Love throughout Freemasonry that it is symbolised on the inside of the bronze doors of the Grand Temple at UGLE. On the left hand door, going out is a man standing holding a lyre, and that is David, on the right hand door is a man standing holding a bow and arrows, and that is Jonathan. This display of the great attribute within Masonic teachings, holds such prominence and is shown in this manner on the very important doors into the Grand Temple.

There are 3 degrees in this wonderful Masonic Order. The first is termed an Induction and the Candidate is introduced by a relating of the situation of David being chosen to be King over Israel after Saul. This is a fascinating degree that has the capacity to lend itself to some amusing moments. It also emphasises the importance of the Almoners role within the Masonic system as this Order has four "Almoners" that are referred to as Visiting Deacons. Each Visiting Deacon is allocated, on average, 25% of the membership with whom he must stay in touch with and enquire about the member's personal well being and that of his wife and family, and ensure that all is well. In other words he must discreetly monitor the safety and well being of his charges. This important element stresses that bit in the title of the Order..... "Brotherhood". By the way, this is the only Masonic Order that has the word Brotherhood in its title.

The second degree, is the "Princes' degree" and the Candidate is Admitted and becomes a member of David's mighty men, and takes the role of one of the Priests sons.

The 3rd degree is the Chair degree, which completes the degrees of this Order. There is much knowledge of the bible stories within this Order that relate the story and life of David, who was the father of Solomon, a character much revered throughout Freemasonry. It is a most enjoyable and happy Order and one much recommended.

Indirectly Attached to this Order is:

CHAPTER 10
THE ANCIENT AND MASONIC ORDER OF THE SCARLET CORD.

This Order relates the story of David sending his spies to gain information about his enemies proposed actions, and carefully explores the bible stories regarding a scarlet woman assisting in the spies' escape, as depicted in the above symbol of the Order. It holds great knowledge of the biblical stories, that adds much to the history of David and his accession to the throne of Israel. As mentioned earlier the importance of this character who was a great friend of Jonathan, as well as being the father of Solomon, is well appreciated throughout freemasonry, and the example of this close friendship is held as a shining example of an important aspect of Freemasonry that it is gloriously displayed for all to see on the doors of the Grand Temple at UGLE.

CHAPTER II
THE WORSHIPFUL SOCIETY OF FREE MASONS, ROUGH MASONS, WALLERS, SLATERS, PAVIORS, PLAISTERERS AND BRICKLAYERS

This is yet another fascinating Order that clearly relates the building of the Temple of King Solomon to that of building the character of a man, and it is done in the most interesting manner that leaves a lasting impression on the Candidate if rightly received and understood. The meetings are held in an Assemblage and are a fantastic study of comparison between a building and a man.

This Order consists of 7 Grades or degrees, numbered accordingly, and each ceremony is a serious study of first, the laying of the foundation stone, up to the placing of the keystone at the top of the building. It exemplifies the work and skill of the artisans that built the Temple of Solomon. It contains much important information and knowledge that will give great understanding not only of the relationship between buildings and man, but will bring a greater depth to the initial degrees of the Craft that all must enter when joining this wonderful Fraternal Society.

CHAPTER 12
GRAND PRIORY OF THE KNIGHTS BENEFICENT OF THE HOLY CITY OF THE RECTIFIED SCOTTISH RITE OF ENGLAND AND WALES.

Scottish Masters of St. Andrew

The Knights Beneficent of the Holy City (KBHC) is the anglicised name of a very old and very "elite" masonic body known worldwide as "CBCS", short for "Chevaliers Bienfaisant de La Cite Sainte".

Recently, in only 2007, the Grand Priory of Belgium sanctioned England to work the Degrees of the Order, forming part of the Rectified Scottish Rite, more openly, but still in a quite restricted, "Invitation Only" manner.

The Scottish Masters of St. Andrew works in the Rectified Scottish Rite. It is an acknowledged fact that admission into the Rectified Scottish Rite is a privilege, which is only extended to brethren of the Temple who have demonstrated, by their general demeanour, and qualities of humility and dignity, that they are worthy of consideration for membership of this elite Christian Order, and must be approved by the Provincial Grand Prior.

The Grand Priory of England is governed by the Grand Master, who is supported by a Grand Prior, a Grand Chancery and a retinue of Grand Officers who are his advisers and assist in the administration of Grand Priory, a meeting of which is convened at least once in every year.

The Prefectures of the Order are administered by a Regional Grand Prefect, who in turn is advised and supported by a Chapter of the Prefecture, which must consist of not less than nine Knights. He is responsible for all activity within the jurisdiction over which he presides. He is empowered to appoint a roll of officers to assist him in the government of the Prefecture. Each Prefecture currently exercises authority over its Lodges of Scottish Masters of St. Andrew.

Degrees of the Rite

The first three degrees of the Rite are synonymous with those of the Craft, which are administered by the Grand Lodge of the respective jurisdiction. The remaining three degrees are conferred under the aegis of the National Grand Priory and comprise:

4. (a) Scottish Master (b) Scottish Master of St. Andrew

These are conferred in a Lodge of St. Andrew by a Worshipful Deputy Master and his team of officers. The degrees collectively embody a revelation that the Temple of the old tradition, also alludes to the treasures revealed through the risen Christ. A regular attendance and a minimum period of at least two years' service is required before a Brother can be considered for advancement into a Chapter of the Interior Order. The aspirant is here elevated to the rank of:

5. Squire Novice

A degree which can be conferred within a Chapter of Squire Novices by the Grand Master or Regional Grand Prefect and officers of the Prefecture. This and the 6th degree are currently performed in a Prefecture. In this degree the aspirant is instructed that it is essential to draw away from the domination of materialism in order to obtain a full and complete understanding of the Supreme Being. A regular attendance as well as a further period of at least two years in that degree must have elapsed before consideration can be given for an Squire Novice to be elevated to the sublime rank of:

6. *Knight Beneficent of the Holy City*

This supreme grade of the Rite is conferred by the Grand Master or Regional Grand Prefect who is empowered by edict of the Grand Master to bestow the accolade. Therein the postulant is exhorted to render due obedience by a faithful observance of God's Law, and that well-informed tolerance, high morals and regular conduct are all necessary qualities for those who seek reception into Knighthood. It embodies the uplifting Ceremony of Armament, of Dubbing and of Consecration, as derived from the general order of Chivalry.

CHAPTER 13
THE HOLY ROYAL ARCH KNIGHT TEMPLAR PRIESTS & ORDER OF HOLY WISDOM.

This Order is a Christian Order and requires you to profess a belief in Jesus Christ and to be a Master Mason, a Companion of the Holy Royal Arch and to be a Knight Templar. It consists of only 2 Degrees namely that of Priest on your Reception and that when you are Installed in the chair.

It also has an Appendant Order called The Order of Holy Wisdom which all members are encouraged to take. There are also 31 other Appendant Orders that are conferred by rote at a particular part of the Reception ceremony. Many of these 31 Appendant Orders are exemplified and notification is sent to all members in order that they may have the opportunity of witnessing the ceremonies and so add to their knowledge of the teachings of this Christian Degree. Whenever one of these Appendant Orders is being conducted invitations are usually sent out inviting members of other Tabernacles to participate.

CHAPTER 14
THE ROYAL ORDER OF SCOTLAND

The Royal Order of Scotland is the oldest Masonic Order, after the Craft, having originated in London in about 1740 and was then re-introduced in Edinburgh in 1763, becoming a Grand Lodge and Chapter in 1767. The Grand Lodge in Edinburgh controls the 90 plus Provincial Grand Lodges situated in many parts of the world. The Order has always claimed that the King of the Scots is the hereditary Grand Master.

There are no individual Lodges or Chapters for the Order only a Provincial Grand Lodge and Chapter for each Province.

With a baseline requirement of five years as a Master Mason, the qualifications for joining this Order vary from Province to Province so it is wise to check with the Province to which you intend to apply.

The Royal Order of Scotland is strictly a Christian Order and its ceremonies are directed to that end..That said, there is firm respectful mention to certain aspects of the Craft, Chapter and other Masonic Orders that perhaps follow a non-Christian path, demonstrating this positive connection across Freemasonry.

There are 2 degrees in this Order, the first being The Royal Order of Heredom of Kilwinning (Provincial Grand Chapter), and the 2nd being the Knighthood of the Rosy

Cross (Provincial Grand Lodge). They are both wonderful degrees with ritual that is conducted in what is referred to as catechetical doggerel and is beautiful to the ear and is delivered totally without the aid of books.

. The Provincial Grand Master is chosen by the Grand Lodge in Edinburgh on submission by the Province.

Like many other Masonic Orders the ritual contained within these ceremonies is wonderful and contains much knowledge and information that proves invaluable to understanding many aspects of your former degrees. The Order is described as "the highest and most sublime degree in Freemasonry", and membership is regarded by many as the pinnacle of their Masonic career.

CHAPTER 15
SOCIETAS ROSICRUCIANA IN ANGLIA

This Order is based on Rosicrucian thought and aspirations, mainly those perpetuated or inspired by Christian Rosenkreutz the acknowledged founder. It is regarded by many to be the portal through to the more Mystical or Esoteric of the Masonic degrees, of which there are many.

The qualification for membership is that you must be a Master Mason under the UGLE. It is primarily a Christian Order and a confirmation of an acceptance of the Holy Trinity is required.

It is a system of 9 grades or degrees, and in each grade there is contained and exemplified a full ceremony that delivers much knowledge about life in all its aspects, religion, the cultures of the world and death. Also many other subjects that affect our lives. Members are encouraged to study the power of numbers, the relevance and symbolism of colours, the various religions of the world, and many other aspects that are an integral part of life.

The units are called Colleges, as each is a place of knowledge and learning. Members are encouraged to produce papers on any chosen subject and present them in open College for the members to discuss and debate. This produces differing subjects and the most lively and enjoyable debates, as you would experience in any regular college.

Progression is as normal as any other Masonic Order, and there is a Provincial unit and also a High Council.

It has been said that not everything is for everybody, and perhaps the keenest of Freemasons who are searching for further light and knowledge are perhaps the most suited for the progress encouraged in this Order.

CHAPTER 16
THE KNIGHT MASONS

The Order of Knight Masons is a chivalric Masonic order, open to all Master Masons who are also members of a Mark Lodge and a Royal Arch Companion, some Councils also require membership of an Allied Masonic Council. Members of the order meet in Councils of Knight Masons which are governed by the Grand Council of Knight Masons based in Dublin, Ireland. A member of the group is a Knight Mason.

The Order of Knight Masons is a system of three degrees, namely Knight of the Sword, Knight of the East, and Knight of the East and West. Councils of Knight Masons are individually presided over by an Excellent Chief and the degrees are conferred separately upon candidates. The Degrees communicate the story of the efforts to build the Second Temple in Jerusalem. They complete the sequence of universal Masonic degrees that are conferred within the Irish system.

Royal Arch and Allied Council members will be fully aware of Zerubbabel's relationship with Cyrus the King of Persia, and later with King Darius, a successor of Cyrus. The 3 degrees of this Order further illustrate in great detail both of these relationships and the events that finally led to the release of the Judean people in Babylon, and their subsequent return to Jerusalem to assist in the glorious work of rebuilding the Temple.

Much of the detail of these 3 ceremonies truly highlight the said relationships of Zerubbabel with Cyrus and then Darius, and subsequently light up much understanding of the Holy Royal Arch. This detail is well worth pursuing and will give great advantage to Companions of the Holy Royal Arch.

CHAPTER 17
THE MASONIC ORDER
OF PILGRIM PRECEPTORS

The Order is based on the story of how Freemasonry came from Jerusalem to England. Candidates are admitted to the degree of Pilgrim, which describes the journey of Freemasonry from Jerusalem to Rome. The second degree is that of Preceptor, and explains the journey from Rome to England. The third degree is the Installation into the chair as an Illustrious Preceptor. The ethos of the Order, and its motto, is "Fraternity, Equality and Liberty". Membership is by invitation, and members must be subscribing Past First Principals of a regular Royal Arch Chapter and subscribing Past Masters of a regular Craft Lodge.

During the late 1870s three Companions conceived the idea of using some of the information they had found in northern Masonic libraries to develop a Masonic ceremony called "the Pilgrim Preceptors", but made no attempt to invite others to join them or to see the ceremony performed. In the 1970s, the son of one of the three conferred the Order on another Companion, who "initiated" five Companions, but nothing more happened until 1984, when the Order was revived and a new ritual produced.

Changes to the Order have been made: the title of units has changed from Preceptory to Conclave, the unit which had originally governed the Order became a Sovereign Grand Conclave and a Time Immemorial Conclave was formed to admit new members. The Order has continued to expand and there are now more than twenty Conclaves in England, USA and Greece.

All companions of the Holy Royal Arch are aware of the First and Holy Lodge, the 2nd or Sacred Lodge and the 3rd or Grand and Royal Lodge, this order of Pilgrim Preceptors is about the 4th and Fraternal Lodge.

In the Holy Royal Arch ritual we learn that in 70 AD Titus the Roman General completely destroyed the Temple and the Jews, in desperation, fled to various parts of the then known world. Some ended up in Rome. The famous catacombs that still exist in Rome is where those Jews held their ceremonies and subsequently formed the Fourth and Fraternal Lodge. Over a short time Titus was convinced of his wrong doing and agreed to allow the Jews more freedom to practice their beliefs. This Order tells this story in a manner that many companions of the Holy Royal Arch may be familiar with. It is well worth furthering your knowledge of this episode in Jewish history.

CHAPTER 18
THE MASONIC ORDER OF ATHELSTAN

The aim of the Masonic Order of Athelstan is to encourage and prompt its members into further study and research. Membership of the Order is strictly invitational, and members are expected to take a wide and committed interest in all aspects of Freemasonry. There is a mandatory requirement for each member to maintain current active membership of both Craft and Royal Arch Masonry. To this end the Order is fully committed to supporting the United Grand Lodge of England and expects all members of the Order to give full support and allegiance to UGLE.

The qualification for becoming a member is that you must be a Subscribing Master Mason and a subscribing Companion of the Holy Royal Arch, as mentioned above.

This Order, the second of only two purely English Masonic Orders in the whole spectrum of Freemasonry, is an invitational Order and its history reflects a particular part of the Anglo Saxon English history. King Athelstan, as well as being a courageous King by ridding our island of the Vikings, he also brought together the many kingdoms ruling various parts of our country to form a united country. He created our laws and coinage. He was the grandson of the legendary King Alfred the Great. In becoming the first King of all the English and being crowned at Kingston, he settled the disputes among the artisan Masons of his time by laying down a set of charges that we in Freemasonry know as "The Ancient Charges". Much of this history is referred to in the "Instruction" of a Candidate when he becomes a member. The ritual and ceremony is quite fantastic culminating in what is referred to as The Circle of Nine where nine of these ancient charges are detailed, and delivered to the candidate in dramatic form. The Masonic units in this Order are called Courts reflecting the royal association of its history and content.

Attached to this Order is a degree of honour which includes aspects of the history of King Alfred the Great and is awarded and conferred by the Grand Court after consultation with the Provincial Grand Master.

This Order does not have any charitable collections, except on nights of Installation when the money collected is for use by the Court Almoner, as it is fully appreciated that much giving is practised in the many other Orders that its members may belong to. The Festive Board operates a similar aspect in so far as the formalities are kept to a polite but respectful minimum so that maximum enjoyment of this special occasion can be greatly appreciated.

This Order affords Freemasons to accent their patriotism, history and Masonic progress in a enjoyable manner.

CHAPTER 19
THE COMMEMORATIVE ORDER OF
St. THOMAS OF ACON

St. Thomas of Acon constituted in 1973 under charter from The Grand Master's Council.

The Order of St. Thomas of Acon was established in 1974 as a result of twenty years' research in the Guildhall Library in London by John E. N. Walker, who for many years was the Secretary General of the Societas Rosicruciana in Anglia. The ancient records of the Order, written in medieval French and Latin, had been deposited in the Guildhall Library and escaped the Great Fire of 1666. The Order now operates under the official title of The Commemorative Order of St. Thomas of Acon.

The Commemorative Order of St. Thomas of Acon is an independent English Christian masonic organisation. Membership is restricted to those who are subscribing members of a Preceptory (Commandery) in amity with the Great Priory of the United Religious, Military and Masonic Order of the Temple of England and Wales and Provinces Overseas (commonly referred to as the Knights Templar). Membership is by invitation only. The basic organisation of the Order is a Chapel.

This Order, as the title suggests, is a commemoration of the life and work of Thomas Becket, who was the son of Gilbert and his wife, a lady he met whilst in the Holy Land assisting in burying the dead. Thomas, as well as attaining to the lofty position of Archbishop of Canterbury in 1162 until his murder in 1170, his work and dedication are exemplified as pure examples of piety and virtue.

The Order illustrates the history of his life and work until his death. It is a very detailed ceremony and one that creates great interest.

Of all the many Orders within the very large Masonic Fraternity there are only 2 Orders that are distinctly English of history and content, and this lovely Order is one of those two.

CHAPTER 20
THE ESOTERIC AND/OR MYSTICAL ORDERS

Within this group of Masonic Orders there are a multitude of units offering a wide range of ceremonies that cover every aspect of history and science, whether real or imagined. In my humble opinion, many of these Orders are to be avoided as they explore aspects that should strongly be interpreted as being certainly not in line with standard Masonic tenets and principles. In the early stages of our career within Freemasonry we are seriously taught many sound principles that will not only benefit our selves, but our neighbours and therefore Society in general. As we progress Masonically, those wonderful Masonic guides to our overall behaviour and regard for others becomes further strengthened. My own personal experience has been to take these Masonic principles and practise them in my everyday life and let them strategically guide me in my progress. In doing this I find that the results have been, and continue to be, extremely rewarding. Not only rewarding but have proved to be a great safeguard soundly reminding me that "*I was taught to be cautious*".

Having said this, it must be acknowledged that a few of the orders I have detailed may not be completely stand alone Orders, and may only be available within a Study or Research group, either way there is tremendous value to be gained in everything that I have included. My intention is not to extort or over encourage joining them, but just to inform the enthusiastic Freemason what is available should he so desire.

In my situation as a Masonic Historian and Lecturer, I felt obliged to join, as much as time and circumstance would allow me, to seek as much knowledge as I could, and indeed it is true to say that I have discovered much knowledge that has yielded me great profit. I have also discovered that there are many more Orders than I can detail in this current book. All the orders that I have joined have required that aspirants must have the benefit of the tenets and principles espoused in mainstream Freemasonry. These principles and tenets have proved their value enabling me to select only those orders and ceremonies that abide by the basic teachings and principles exemplified within mainstream Freemasonry. They remain my foundation stone and I cannot recommend strongly enough that the eager Freemason adopt similar guidelines.

In the early days of Freemasonry a prolific number of rituals were created, and during a regular Lodge meeting chosen aspirants would be called to the side of the Lodge room and were indoctrinated into the new Order. Hence the title "Side Orders". Some of those old orders have faded, but many have either continued to exist or had their ritual including their message and teachings revived. They have much useful information and knowledge and for the aspiring Freemason further satisfaction in working with likeminded individuals.

Many of the esoteric or mystical Orders practise white magic, theurgic magic, meditative experiences, and invocations of a powerful nature. Should any of these practises be abused or mishandled, one does not know how dangerous the outcome could be, and it is certainly not an experience I would like to have.

If involved in an Order that has strong invocations that might have a tendency to open up the mind, and you have say a dozen members involved with these situations, their attitude and spiritual strength should be fairly equal in approach and reasonably well balanced. There could be good influences coming into the atmosphere invoked, but there could also be bad influences as well. Unless the unified spiritual strength is equal, knowledge of what bad influence may invade the open mind is unknown, so that when you wish to close the session down with reverse invocations, the trouble has already been done, and the mind closes with the bad influence shut in the mind, and the manner in which it might manifest itself is also unknown.

I have only joined units of this nature when I know that there are already a majority of sensible members that fully subscribe to the above mentioned Masonic principles.

It is akin to having 12 batteries that are attached to each other. If all are working fine and are of equal power then you will achieve the level of power that you want. But if one or two are not working to their full extent, then you are temporarily ignorant of what may happen, or what may NOT happen. This analogy is of consequence for the spiritual energy of the individual encouraged by invocations or physical supplications, is simply that.....it is ENERGY, precisely as the electricity of a group of batteries is ENERGY. The one thing that does not die is ENERGY, that is a scientific fact.

Esoteric and or Mystical study may not be for everyone. For those who wish to pursue this path, and it is most enjoyable for those so inclined. Should be cautious in their approach to them and ensure that they will be comfortable within that atmosphere.

Having expressed much caution I will now continue with my explanations of some of these more serious mystical/esoteric Orders.

·   RWH

CHAPTER 21
THE HERMETIC ORDER OF MARTINISTS

Martinism is a form of an initiatic esoteric or mystical Christianity that regards Jesus Christ as The Repairer and aims for the reintegration of man to attain an idealised state. Such a state aimed for is that in the Garden of Eden before the Fall of Man as described in the Holy Bible (Genesis 3, 1 – 6

Martinism reflects the philosophy and esoteric Christian mysticism of the French philosopher Louis Claude de Saint-Martin (1743 – 1803), who was a disciple of the 18th century Freemason and theurgist, Martinez de Pasqually (1727 – 1774). Saint-Martin's spiritual writings were published under his pseudonym of "Le Philosophe Inconnu", or the "Unknown Philosopher".

The Hermetic Order of Martinists (HOM) is only open to Master Masons of a Lodge under the authority of the United Grand Lodge of England, or of a Grand Lodge recognised by them. It is required that aspirants have a Trinitarian Christian Belief. Some units require you to be a member of the SRIA.

By a process of initiation, meditation, study, esoteric discussion and contemplation, members of the Order aim to discover and understand the presence of Jesus Christ within. The Order is organised on a Lodge system similar to that of Freemasonry. A Heptad is composed of a minimum of seven members and a Lodge has a minimum of 21 members.

A Circle has less than seven members. Meetings are known as Conventicles.

There are three grades, or degrees in the system of the Hermetic Order of Martinists:

- First Degree: Associate.
- Second Degree: Initiate
- Third Degree: *Supérieur Inconnu*, SI or Unknown Superior.

This Order is a truly esoteric Order and is one of deep philosophical study. Its ritual contains all the elements required for deep meditation and papers are presented and discussed. No general Lodge business is conducted within the actual meeting as mundane matters would corrupt the meditative processes. The joint 'supper' is where the mundane business is conducted and a discussion on some esoteric or mystical subject is debated.

Because of the content and format of the meetings of this Order the reason that a grounding in the SRIA in some cases is preferred, is completely understandable.

RWH

CHAPTER 22
THE MASONIC ORDER OF THE ELUS COHEN

The Élus Coëns (Elect Priest) is an Esoteric Christian order founded in 1767, with its focus on establishing an invisible church, independent of any earthly structure, (That Temple not made with hands, eternal in the Heavens) to find the path that leads to the hidden knowledge of nature in anticipation of the coming destruction of the material Church. That is to say, by a progressive initiation and a direct knowledge of God to obtain the primordial unity, which was lost since the fall of Adam – the Reintegration – through the practice of theurgy, which relied on complex ceremonial practices aimed at what Pasqually termed the reconciliation of the 'minor' person with Divinity. This was to be accomplished through human communication with the angelic hierarchies. In other words, they practised theurgy which consisted of evoking the intermediary spirits, such as angels and celestial beings in order to obtain their help and support. With this in mind, the Masonic system provides an adequate structure for this course taken using occultist methods.

The teachings address essentially major themes relating to the Judeo-Christian tradition, but from an esoteric point of view, under the Cabbalistic and Valentinian-gnostic influences found in Pasqually's own texts, rituals and catechisms. They drew upon the power of Church prayers, banishing the influence of Satan from humanity.

"An order that, having for goal to bring man back to his glorious origin, leads him by the hand, by teaching him to know himself and to consider his relationships with the entire nature, of which he was to be the centre had he not fallen from his origin, and finally to recognise the Supreme Being from which he is emanated."

Papus

This Order is quite serious in its content and aims and attracts the more serious applicants. It is wise to have a background of the principles of mainstream Freemasonry, experience of the SRIA, and possibly involvement with the Hermetic Order of Martinism. As I have mentioned earlier it is wise to possess some knowledge and experience of safeguards when anticipating entry into this type of esoteric pursuit, and there are none better than those inculcated in Freemasonry etc.

Its structure and progress is very similar to many effected in Freemasonry. From entry one can aspire right up to Grand Master Cohen 9°.

CHAPTER 23
THE AUGUST ORDER OF LIGHT

This society of Freemasons supplies a series of grades and possesses rituals which illustrate the Old World Religions, and notably the mythologies of India, with sidelights from the cults of Ancient Egypt, Greece and Rome. While the Rosicrucian Society illustrates the teachings of the Mystics of the Middle Ages of Europe, this Order gives a view of Oriental ideas of Theology and Cosmogony.

The August Order of Light is not essentially an Esoteric Order but more a mystical one as it takes much of its content from what are known as the Ancient mysteries.

The August Order of Light seeks to explain the symbolism of Craft Freemasonry by reference to the old world religions particularly the mythologies of India, Ancient Greece and Rome. The Order is not adding to or replacing the ritual of Craft Freemasonry, but providing keys to explain it. It is the ardent aim "that all members will receive some degree of illumination from participating in the mysteries of the Order, thus rending the veil of darkness between the physical and spiritual planes".

Meetings are held in a Ashayana as opposed to a Lodge or Temple.

It is a fascinating Order that studies many aspects of our universe, and aspects that control our universe such as the stars and planets, the seasons and the solstices, the signs of the zodiac. All of that, and its attached relevance's, which appear to have been much better appreciated and understood by the Ancients of many cultures.

Membership is by strict invitation only. It is also desired that an involvement in Rosicrucianism an advantage as it will enable aspirants to take so much more of what the Order has to offer. Before full acceptance Aspirants must deliver a prepared paper in front of a committee of members in order to prove worthiness.

CHAPTER 24
THE ANCIENT AND ARCHAEOLOGICAL ORDER
OF DRUIDS OR THE ORDER OF TALIESIN

Meetings of Druids are held in a GROVE, whereas they used to always be held in the open air, most often now they are held in the more convenient, comfortable and warmer surroundings of a temple lending a more stable atmosphere to the meeting. Days of meetings in cold damp muddy fields or woods are fading fast. The symbolism and meaning of the ceremonies are still maintained with the fullest energy of the participants.

Druidry is an acknowledgement that the individual is an integral part of total Creation. The ceremonies include not only the duty of responsibility and stewardship, but are also a serious gesture of gratitude and appreciation to the Creator. Bearing in mind this important ethos, aspirants are encouraged to find their particular part in the overall scheme of all things, accept their duties of stewardship, and enjoy being a part of a discipline that has existed for thousands of years.

The only thing new about "Eco-Warriors" is their title. Protection of and respect for our planet and all that is involved for its perfect survival is proving, in these modern times, to be of paramount importance.

An order, although reflecting back to some of our earliest ancestors and, inculcating identical standards of moral judgement and appreciation for our natural surroundings, in these modern times has more direct connections than what was formerly understood and appreciated. When these concepts are exemplified in an atmosphere closely related to those of strong Masonic ceremonies, the wider circle of everything in the universe comes fully together.

CHAPTER 25
THE MYSTERIES OF MITHRAS

The Mysteries of Mithras is an independent order which is inspired by and uses the allegory of the lost and ancient Mysteries of the previously influential Roman Cult of the same name. The Order is open to all Master Masons who are members in good-standing and governed or recognised by the United Grand Lodge of England.

However, the Mysteries of Mithras is not an historical re-enactment, nor a religious order and there is no requirement for any specific religious belief for membership, with the ceremonies being compatible with all members' personal faiths. There is no claim to have direct lineal descent from the original mystery cults of ancient Rome. Instead, inspiration is taken from and based on the allegorical grades of the Order and on the teachings and symbols of the Mysteries of Mithras.

The Order's objective is to bring together Brethren with an inquisitive and philosophical view on Freemasonry, who wish to learn more about themselves and the hidden Mysteries of Mithras. All aspiring candidates who are seeking to make a daily advancement in Masonic knowledge are invited to knock on the door of the Mysteries and enquire about the anciently inspired rituals.

Their meetings are intended to be thought-provoking and enjoyable experiences for brethren who are genuinely interested in extending their Masonic knowledge and who enjoy stimulating and allegorical Masonic ritual. Again this is not what one would regard as an Esoteric Order but it has the excellence of ceremony that will promote thought and debate. The after meeting Feast continues in the Mithraic tradition.

There are 7 grades from "Corax" up to "The Trial of Pater" (The Father). The rituals reflect the real atmosphere of the mysteries of this originally Persian belief system, that was later adopted by the Romans extensively throughout the Empire. The Romans had a Mithraic Temple or Mithraeum in the City of London, which was excavated in the 1960's and is now an historic site that you can visit and tour around.

The are seven grades or trials in the Mysteries of Mithras, must be taken in order. The first four are known as the "Terrestrial Grades" and grades five to seven are referred to as the "Celestial Grades". When an initiate join's he will take the First Grade or the Trial of Corax. This ceremony will introduce the initiate to the Order as well as delving into the meaning of the Mysteries and creation myth of the Universe.

Grades; two, three and four (Nymphus, Miles & Leo) are taken separately but form a trilogy, with Mithras going on a journey of self-discovery. The candidate will venture on a quest very much in the style of that of the ancient Roman and Greek myths. With all of the ceremonies in the Order, the Fraters are encouraged to participate and play an active role in the rituals; allowing every Frater to be involved and to experience the ceremonies after having gone through them.

I will not go into too much detail on the content of the celestial grades at this stage, for fear of giving too much away - which must be earnt. However, the grades are The Trial of Perses and the Trial of Heliodromas with the final grade of the Order being that of The Trial of the Pater - which is very much the equivalent of the Worshipful Master of the Legion.

CHAPTER 26
THE ROYAL ORDER OF ERI

This remote and elite Order is said to be derived from a very ancient Order in Ireland, consisting of freemasons and said to have been erected and patronised by the Kings of Ireland, for it is claimed that in early times Erin (Ireland) possessed a literature and history equal to that of the most highly developed of ancient nations. While it is generally accepted that Bro John Yarker (1833 – 1913) was at one time head of the 'English Revived Order of the Red Branch of Eri', certain records of the Order relate that Bro F. G. Irwin, while Worshipful Master of the Inhabitants Lodge No 178 at Gibraltar in 1858, received the Order at the hands of the captain of an American trading vessel, to whom it had been transmitted from father to son, dating back to 1757, when his Irish forbear emigrated to New York while a District Grand Master of the Order. Major Irwin is then purported to have restored and reorganised the degree in England under the aegis of the Grand Mur-Ollamham. The order possesses two Psalters, the Major Psalter being basically the rituals of the degrees and the Minor Psalter comprising the laws and rules of the order.

Admission to this order is strictly by invitation only and is restricted to members of the Societas Rosicruciana in Anglia who have attained the fifth grade or above. The Order is governed by a Most Enlightened Grand Master who is supported by eight Knights Grand Cross and also a retinue of hierarchy designated Ard Officers who constitute the Grand Mur-Ollamham.

The degrees embodied in this Order are:

1. *Man-at-Arm*s: The candidate is admitted under an exhortation of a celebrated Celtic Bard by the name of Mac Leag (AD 1015) and in a simple yet impressive ceremony, is duly armed.

2. *Esquire*: Reception into the second degree is promulgated through the interpretation of an important charge which stimulates the candidate to demonstrate humility and service in supporting the honourable creed of the ancient kings.

3. *Knight*: In this, the last degree, the aspirant is encouraged to engage in figurative combat and his reward is the acclaim of his Brother Knights, to commemorate the mighty deeds of their forbears at the Battle of Ossary. After investiture he is instructed in the Ancient Mysteries and Legends of the Order by the Brehon.

There are three Chapters of the Order; meeting in London and the Midlands as well as in Australia.

(This extract is from the Web).

CHAPTER 27
THE MARTINIST ORDER OF SPIRITUAL KNIGHTS

This Order is by a very strict invitation only and only Master Masons who are already Martinists are allowed to take advantage of this rare invite, should it come their way. It is a very powerful Christian Order where the aspirant declares that he is searching for a higher wisdom or what becomes known as The True Light.

Ivan Jean Vladimirovich Lopukhin 1756-1816, was a Russian Martinist, Philosopher, Educator, Writer, Publisher and Philanthropist.

Ivan Vladimirovich Lopukhin, the originator of this Martinist Christian Order, was born on the 24th February 1756 in the Village of Voskresenskoye in the province of Orel into a wealthy family of landowners of the upper nobility. Lopukhin was plagued by a sickly childhood and he received much of his education at home. At the age of nineteen (1775), he began his military service with the Preobrazhensky Regiment, however, due to his health, he retired seven years later with the rank of Colonel. Lopukhin was a keen student of law, and in 1782 was appointed as counsellor of the Moscow Criminal Court, later he was to become the court President.

Lopukhin's chief interest in judicial affairs was the reformatory aspects of the law, he once wrote that it was better to acquit many criminals than to convict one innocent individual, this progressive stance resulted in a dispute with J. A. Bruce the conservative Governor-General of Moscow, this lead to Lopukhin's forced resignation in 1785.

Lopukhin, thereafter, assumed and active role in the literary and philanthropic activities of Nikolaj Ivanovich Novikov (1744-1818) the prominent Martinist and Rosicrucian. In 1789 while recovering from a lengthy period of illness Lopukhin underwent a religious conversion and embraced a particular blend of Martinism, Rosicrucianism and Masonry as a new, spiritual and idealistic world-view.

He became Grandmaster of a Masonic Lodge in Moscow, he also translated the works of Western mystics and Freemasons, and wrote several treatises of his own, In 1790, he published a defence of Masonry in Russia that called for love of God and one's fellow man and for constant inner and personal improvement called "Nravouchitelnyi Katezhizis Istinnykh Franmasonov"

During Catherine the Great's campaign to rid Russia of the notorious new schism of Freemasonry, Lopukhin was searched and questioned for his Masonic activities and was arrested in 1792, and sent to Siberia.

The Empress relented and allowed him to stay in Moscow for the sake of his ageing father, Lopukhin lived in Moscow from 1792-1796 and wrote and published many literary and dramatic works. In 1796, when Tsar Paul, who was also a Freemason assumed the throne, he acquitted Novikov and recognising Lopukhin's talents and abilities his career in the Russian Civil Service resumed, he was summoned to St. Petersburg and was appointed State Secretary, the following year, Lopukhin returned to Moscow as a Senator.

A prominent theme in many of Lopukhin's writings was the idea of a spiritual "inner church", the enemies of which were the secular learning and self-indulgence which kept man from following Christ and gaining "true wisdom".

Lopukhin's ideal man, the "spiritual knight", was one

who defended the "inner church" with the spiritual weapons of silent suffering and freely given love. In the essay "Glas Iskrennosti", Lopukhin had characterized the Doukhobors as the "hidden saints" of his new church, perhaps the most famous convert to his idea of a new inner church was Leo Tolstoy, who became an archetype of Lopukhin's "spiritual knight". Tolstoy with his "conversion" to a new non-doctrinal Christianity that abjured violence and taught that "the kingdom of God is within you", would, like Lopukhin before him, view the Doukhobors as living examples of this philosophical ideal.

On the 22nd June 1816, Lopukhin died at his family estate.

He had enjoyed great popularity among his contemporaries, was thought of as the epitome of the fair and disinterested judge and philanthropist, a man who put the welfare of his Motherland before his own, and a trusted advisor to the Tsars, however, his mystic writings and philosophy earned him many denigrators who accused him of hypocrisy and personal defects.

Sadly, due to his role and influence in the history of the Doukhobors, and perhaps second only to Tolstoy amongst "outsiders" to the sect, he remains largely unappreciated and forgotten. Lopukhin's spiritual legacy continues however, through the Russian and Ukrainian lineages.

(This extract is taken from the history portrayed in the actual ritual book of the Order).

CHAPTER 28
THE ILLUMINATI

This Order has attracted suspicion, notoriety, speculation also ill-found fame at the hands of sensationalist writers like Dan Brown, whether as novels or based on supposed facts. The original Order deserves none of this type of popular media crassness.

The ethos of the original Order was to bring peace and harmony to the world through the means of education and knowledge in a manner based on the original simple principles of the main religions and belief systems of the world. Not too far removed from the teachings of Freemasonry. The so called modern world of those times had become obsessed with itself and was being guided by egoists and self interested profiteering so-called pragmatists. The Illuminati was/is simply a society formed to "return to basics", to stabilize society and re-direct the wealth more evenly. At that time to propose and attempt to create their objectives things had to be done in secret, by a group of extremely like minded knowledgeable men from various areas across society. The Church being all powerful, any doctrine that was preached or taught that appeared to threaten the supremacy of the Church was put down immediately with violence if necessary. So the meetings were held in secret, and after a time, as history has proved, secrecy becomes the bed for malicious rumour and dangerous speculation. This sort of dangerous speculation builds upon itself and reaches a peak so that the original concept becomes totally suffocated and the wild speculation becomes the reality.

The title of the Order is much misunderstood. It simply means "Light" and light means knowledge and understanding, much like we understand its concept in modern Freemasonry. Even in cartoons when the character perceives a good idea a light bulb appears over his head. Even when we ourselves have a "Eureka" moment we claim that we have "seen the light". Jesus himself is sometimes portrayed as the "Light".

Originally formed by Adam Weishaupt on 1st May 1776 in Bavaria, Germany. The society's goals were to oppose superstition, obscurantism, religious influence over public life, and abuses of state power. "The order of the day," they wrote in their general statutes, "is to put an end to the machinations of the purveyors of injustice, to control them without dominating them." Historically, the name usually refers to the Bavarian Illuminati, an Enlightenment-era secret society founded by Adam Weishaupt. The society's goals were to oppose superstition, obscurantism, religious influence over public life, and abuses of state power. "The order of the day," they wrote in their general statutes, "is to put an end to the machinations of the purveyors of injustice, to control them without dominating them." The Illuminati — along with Freemasonry and other secret societies — were outlawed through edict by Charles Theodore, Elector of Bavaria with the encouragement of the Catholic Church, in 1784, 1785, 1787, and 1790. In the following several years, the group was vilified by conservative and religious critics who claimed that they continued underground and were responsible for the French Revolution, an accusation also aimed at Freemasonry over the years.

The rituals of the Society were deemed lost but were

much later found buried deep in some Masonic archives, having been translated by Arthur Edward Waite. They are now worked and celebrated for their content, principles and obvious connected historic value.

So far the invitation is strictly limited and usually applies only to senior Rosicrucians. Much in line with the original concepts.

CHAPTER 29
THE SWEDENBORG RITE

The Swedenborg Rite or Rite of Swedenborg was a fraternal order modelled on Freemasonry and based upon the teachings of Emanuel Swedenborg. It comprised six Degrees: Apprentice, Fellow Craft, Master Neophyte, Illuminated Theosophite, Blue Brother, and Red Brother.[

It was created in Avignon in 1773 by the Marquis de Thorn. It was initially a political organization, whose aims might bring freemasonry into disrepute, although the political ideology was eventually discarded from the rite. [2] This version of the Swedenborg Rite died out within a decade of its founding.

Starting in the 1870s, the Rite was resurrected as an hermetic organization. This version faded out sometime around 1908.[3] In 1982 a patent of the Swedenborg Rite was transmitted by the English Freemason Desmond Bourke, in his office at the British Museum, to Masonic author Michele Moramarco, who after revising the rituals by Bourke's permission revived that tradition in Italy under the title of "Antico Rito Noachita" ("Ancient Noachide Rite") .

(Some info on Emmanuel Swedenborg).

Emanuel Swedenborg, a distinguished theologian of his age, and the founder of a sect which still exists, has been always mythically connected with Freemasonry. The eagerness is indeed extraordinary with which all Masonic writers, German, French, English, and American, have sought to connect the name and labors of the Swedish sage with the Masonic institution, and that, too, without the slightest foundation for such a theory either in his writings, or in any Credible memorials of his life.

Findel (History of Freemasonry, page 329), speaking of the reforms in Swedish Freemasonry, says: "Most likely Swedenborg, the mystic and visionary, used his influence in bringing about the new system; at all events, he smoothed the way for it." Lenning speaks of the influence of his teachings upon the Swedish system of Freemasonry, although he does not absolutely claim him as a Freemason.

Reghellini, in his *Esprit du Dogme de la Franche Maçonnerie*, or Genius of the Tenets of Freemasonry, writes thus: "Swedenborg made many very learned researches on the subject of the Masonic mysteries. He thought that their doctrines were of the highest antiquity, having emanated from the Egyptians, the Persians, the Magi, the Jews, and the Greeks.

He also became the head of a new religion in his effort to reform that of Rome. For this purpose he wrote his Celestial Jerusalem, or his Spiritual World: he mingled with his reform, ideas which were purely Masonic. In this celestial Jerusalem the Word formerly communicated by God to Moses is found; this word is Jehovah, lost on earth, but which he invites us to find in Great Tartary, a Country still governed, even in our days, by the patriarchs, by which he means allegorically to say that this people most nearly approach to the primitive condition of the perfection of innocence." But there is no work written by Swedenborg which bears either of those titles, Celestial Jerusalem or Spiritual World. It is possible that Reghellini alludes either to the Arcana Celestia, published in 1749-53, or to the De Nova Hierosolyma, published in 1758. The same writer, in his *Maçonnerie considérée comme le résultat des religions*

Egyptienne, Juive et Chrétienne, or 'Masonry considered as the result of Egyptian, Jewish, and Christian Religions' (ii, page 454), repeatedly speaks of Swedenborg as a Masonic reformer, and sometimes as a Masonic impostor. Ragon also cites Reghellini in his *Orthodoxe Maçonnique* (page 255), and recognizes Swedenborg as the founder of a Masonic system.

This order is currently conducted and researched by students of Freemasonry purely for historical purposes.

CHAPTER 30
THE SACRED AND NOBLE ORDER OF
THE KNIGHTS OF CORVIDA

The Purpose of the Order is for its members to attain to a better understanding of life in its present phase and to study the lesser known laws of nature in order to obtain some understanding of life as it will be, when the process of evolution has carried the development of the species of life to a more advanced level than the present phase. To understand the statement better, it is necessary to discuss briefly the fundamental principles upon which the philosophy of the Knights Corvida rest. For example, the Sign of the Corvida is the figure of a bird with wings outstretched – sometimes shown in black - at other times it is shown in gold. The bird represents the lifting up out of our present condition of evolution into a higher stage. The Sign in black represents this process of advancement gradually taking place without our conscious knowledge. The Sign - gold represents this process taking place within our conscious knowledge. This brings us to the problem of the nature of being and existence.

The Knights Corvida holds to the view that the basic concepts of life are the principles of Space, Time and Consciousness. This is a continuum, each concept or principle being, in fact, an aspect of the other two. It is possible to suppose that Space and Time can exist independently of consciousness but it has not been, nor can it be, demonstrated that this is so, as every demonstration rests upon the presence of conscious activity for its manifestation. Whatever events occur in the Universe can only be known to us in relation to the degree of our awareness.

Again this Order is one of Strict invitation and is only suitable to aspirants who may wish to investigate and follow this philosophy

CHAPTER 31
THE MASONIC ORDER OF ST. PATRICK

The Order of Saint Patrick was instituted by King George III of England in the year 1783, for the valuable assistance rendered him by the courageous Knights of Erie. This Order was Christian in nature and the symbol of Ireland was adopted as the Jewel of the Order. Saint Patrick, being held in high veneration, was made the patron Saint, his life being one of service to God and his fellowmen.

Saint Patrick, in order to teach the Oneness of the Triune God, used the Shamrock because of its natural formation, to show that God is three persons in one – Father, Son and Holy Ghost. He spent his early boyhood as a shepherd and during this period, much of his time was spent in prayer. As he prayed faithfully, the Great Commandment became clear to him and became part of his future life and service.

In the latter days of his life Saint Patrick wrote these words which seem to summarise his entire life; (Daily I expect either a violent death or to be robbed and reduced to slavery or the occurrence of some such calamity. I have cast myself into the hands of God, for He rules everything).

This was apparently the secret of the inexhaustible courage and determination that prevailed throughout his life. Hence God and Service became the theme of this Order, which has lain dormant these many years, and takes life into the twenty-first Century.

You only have to be a Master Mason to enjoy this charming and beautiful Order.

CHAPTER 32
THE ORDER OF THE FRATRES LUCIS

When it was founded the ORDO Fratres Lucis or order of the Brothers of the light, it was not a reference to the Illuminati order of Adam Weishaupt founded in 1776. It was inspired by the Florentine order of the Brothers of the Light, founded in 1498, as a secret continuation of the Platonic Academy of Marcelo Ficcino.

This order is not affiliated with the material plan to any order or fraternity initiatory, although on the spiritual level it shares the high ideals of esoteric orders and fraternities, such as Rosicrucianism, Martinism and Freemasonry.

The School of Mysteries is called the Order of the "Fratres Lucis" or "Order of the Brothers of the Light". In Latin, it's the ORDO fratres Lucis. This order, like every initiatory order, has its temples (shops) that are the physical meeting places of its members. The incorporation of one of them requires the respective initiation in the first degree of the Ordo fratres Lucis, and the material sustenance of the said temple is like any other material organization, but in this case, the quotas are fixed by each store independently, dues or contributions to the order, that is, will only be for the sustenance of its structure and materials.

Another fantastic Order little known and therefore little practised, but its content not only continues the ethos of many of the more established esoteric orders, but assists the aspirant to gain much about himself and the natural world about him and as a consequence a greater appreciation of everything is the profit yielded.

CHAPTER 33
THE ANCIENT AND NOBLE ORDER
OF THE ESSENES

This order is ideal for those of a particular strong religious belief that Christianity in its purest form emanated from this elite Jewish community and was interpreted much later as not being simply another Jewish sect, but more a way of life and belief standing apart from the standard Jewish faith prevalent in those times. There are many connections for this plausible conclusion. And now for some of those connections.

The Essenes were members of an ascetic Jewish sect of the 1st century BC and the 1st century AD. Most of them lived on the western shore of the Dead Sea. They are identified by many scholars with the Qumran community that wrote the documents popularly called the Dead Sea Scrolls. They numbered about 4,000 members. Admission required two to three years of preparation, and new candidates took an oath of piety, justice, and truthfulness.

According to Philo of Alexandria and other writers of the 1st century AD, the Essenes shared their possessions, lived by agriculture and handicrafts, rejected slavery, and believed in the immortality of the soul. Their meals were solemn community affairs. The main group of Essenes opposed marriage. They had regular prayer and study sessions, especially on the Sabbath. Transgressors were excluded from the sect.

The similarity between a number of Essene and Christian concepts and practices (kingdom of God, baptism, sacred meals, the position of a central teacher, titles of officeholders, and community organization) has led many people to assume that there was a close kinship between the Essenes and the groups around John the Baptist and Jesus Christ. It is possible that after the dissolution of the Essene community some members followed John the Baptist or joined one of the early Christian communities,

"Essenes" is an English transliteration of the Greek Essenoi. The derivation and meaning of the Greek word have been a mystery since the first century A.D. Philo, our earliest source (ca. A.D. 40), speculated that "Essenes" was derived from the Greek hosios, meaning "holy." Modern scholars have preferred to go back to Semitic originals. The two most probable etymologies offered to date are from the Aramaic 'asen,' asayya, "healers," and from the East Aramaic hasen, hasayya, "the pious." The first etymology would suggest a link between the Essenes and the Therapeutae (Gr. "healers"), a similar Jewish group flourishing contemporaneously in Egypt. The second etymology would imply a historical relationship between the Essenes and the Hasidim (Hebrew: "pious ones"), the faithful Jews who distinguished themselves during the Maccabean revolt (ca. 167 B.C.). Extant evidence will not allow a firm decision between the two etymologies, though it would seem that the latter currently enjoys more credence. In any case, there is no reason to assume that "Essenes," or Semitic equivalent, was a self-designation. It may have been a label applied to the group by outsiders. As such, it would point to the manner in which the Essenes were perceived by their contemporaries.

Josephus in his writings claims that Essenes are the followers of Essa. Now this proves highly interesting as the name "ESSA" is such as is applied to Jesus in the Koran.

So Josephus claims that the Essenes are followers of Jesus. Now this brings a heavy question on the chronology, but this can be erased and solved if you subscribe to the opinions of that eminent academic and biblical scholar David Rohl with his excellent conclusions in his book "*A Test of Time*".

It is acknowledged by many bible academics that the time spent by Jesus "In the Wilderness" was time spent at Qumran with the Essenes, as the teachings of Christ through the parables and the sermon on the mount, are identical with Essenic teachings and principles.

It is highly possible, and indeed most likely, that pilgrims and especially crusaders came across these teachings and adopted them for themselves or their groups and practiced them secretly as the dominance of the Catholic Church was all powerful and their treatment of such "heresy" was death.

It may be from these circumstances that this ritual has come down to us, or most likely these fine principles have been maintained in a dramatic form in the pious memory of those estimable Jews known as THE ESSENES.

Which ever way you choose to believe is of no real consequence, what is of consequence is the real enjoyment you will obtain from the beauty of this ritual and the principles it portrays.

CHAPTER 34
THE ANCIENT AND HEROIC ORDER OF THE GORDIAN KNOT.

The Ancient and Heroic Order of the Gordian Knot was instituted by Alexander of Macedonia in 334 B. C. It flourished until the year 1071 A. D. when the Turkish conquerors eradicated every trace of the old Order --- or so they thought. Although history books refer to the Order of the Gordian Knot, it was generally believed that no written records of the Order had escaped the devastating hands of the Turks. In the year 1957 an ancient scroll was discovered containing the entire ritual of the Order, written in the hand of Arrian, Alexander's historian. It has been faithfully translated from the original Greek into English and the Order has been revived by the Supreme Grand Synod of the Ancient and Heroic Order of the Gordian Knot.

This ritual is based upon two incidents which occurred when Alexander the Great set forth upon his conquest of Persia, accompanied by an army of 50,000 infantry and cavalry. One of his generals, Parmenion, intercepted a traitorous communication from the Son of Aeropos, one of Alexander's closest friends, to Darius, King of Persia in which the Son of Aeropos offered to assassinate Alexander if Darius would pay him well and assist him in ascending the throne following Alexander's death. Darius accepted the proposal and offered the Son of Aeropos a reward of 10,000 Talents for Alexander's death.

The manner in which this information was communicated to King Alexander and the action taken against the traitor is revealed as an important part of the ceremonies of the Order in which candidates are about to be received. In this ceremony it will be necessary for the candidate to take the part of the traitor and to suffer the same penalty suffered by the infamous Son of Aeropos. Expressing a willingness to undergo the trial the candidate is blindfolded, the traditional manner in which traitors were led before the King, with the assurance that, if a successful pass through the rigours of initiation is achieved, the candidate will be elevated to full membership as a Companion of the Ancient and Heroic Order of the Gordian Knot.

The Gordian Knot is a legend of Phrygian Gordium associated with Alexander the Great. It is often used as a metaphor for an intractable problem (untying an impossibly-tangled knot) solved easily by finding an approach to the problem that renders the perceived constraints of the problem moot ("cutting the Gordian knot"):

At one time the Phrygians were without a king. An oracle at Telmissus (the ancient capital of Phrygia) decreed that the next man to enter the city driving an ox-cart should become their king. A peasant farmer named Gordias drove into town on an ox-cart. His position had also been predicted earlier by an eagle landing on his cart, a sign to him from the gods, and on entering the city Gordias was declared king by the priests. Out of gratitude, his son Midas dedicated the ox-cart to the Phrygian god Sabazios (whom the Greeks identified with Zeus) and either tied it to a post or tied its shaft with an intricate knot of cornel (*Cornus mas*) bark. The ox-cart still stood in the palace of the former kings of Phrygia at Gordium in the fourth century BC when Alexander arrived, at which point Phrygia had been reduced to a satrapy, or province, of the Persian Empire.

Several themes of myth converged on the chariot, as Midas was connected in legend with Alexander's native Macedonia, where the lowland "Gardens of Midas" still bore his name, and the Phrygian tribes were rightly remembered as having once dwelt in Macedonia. So, in 333 BC, while wintering at Gordium, Alexander the Great attempted to untie the knot. When he could not find the end to the knot to unbind it, he sliced it in half with a stroke of his sword, producing the required ends (the so-called "Alexandrian solution"). That night there was a violent thunderstorm. Alexander's prophet Aristander took this as a sign that Zeus was pleased and would grant Alexander many victories. Once Alexander had sliced the knot with a sword-stroke, his biographers claimed in retrospect that an oracle further prophesied that the one to untie the knot would become the king of Asia.

Alexander is a figure of outstanding celebrity and the dramatic episode with the Gordian Knot remains widely known. Literary sources are Alexander's propagandist Arrian (Anabasis Alexandri) Quintus Curtius, Justin's epitome of Pompeius Trogus), and Aelian's De Natura Animalium. While sources from antiquity agree that Alexander was confronted with the challenge of the knot, the means by which he solved the problem are disputed. Both Plutarch and Arrian relate that according to Aristobulus, Alexander pulled the knot out of its pole pin, exposing the two ends of the cord and allowing him to untie the knot without having to cut through it. Some classical scholars regard this as more plausible than the popular account. Alexander later went on to conquer Asia as far as the Indus and the Oxus thus, for Callisthenes, fulfilling the prophecy.

Knowing the incredible exploits and achievements of Alexander the Great it comes as no surprise that researchers have delved into his ancient history and created such an inspiring ceremony. This ceremony enacts a part of ancient history that is in a small way reasonably well known, but its actual intricacies are much less appreciated. The ceremony also lends itself to some light-hearted moments.

CHAPTER 33
STUDY GROUPS AND STUDY CIRCLES.

These have become very popular over the past few years. They are privately run, there is no hierarchy, no Grand jurisdiction or Provincial jurisdiction. Therefore without dues, donations and expensive meals or administration costs to consider they are truly economic. There are a few of this type of group scattered around. I can really only speak of the two that I belong to. ı is in Sutton, Surrey and the one I run is in Chatham, Kent. They both work along the same lines.

Only true Freemasons under UGLE are admitted. Regalia is limited to a white alb and Cordelier. Costs for the hire of the hall and light meal are requested, and are usually very cheap. The ceremonies vary from meeting to meeting depending on what the membership request and wish to experience and discuss. The furniture for each ceremony varies from ritual to ritual and is usually obtained from boot fairs and the like, or whatever can be cannibalised. There are no certificates or records indicating progress or attendance. Members are simply interested in working the old ceremonies, obtaining the knowledge they may contain and discussing the value of the ceremony and its content. After the ceremony Candidates are usually presented with the ritual in order that they can make further study in their own time. It is my experience that there is much to be appreciated contained in these apparently defunct rituals.

This is an opportunity for the most ardent Brethren to further their Masonic interests in a friendly and economic manner and gain much knowledge from these ancient and valued Masonic rituals.

CHAPTER 34
CLOSING COMMENTS

Although I have given details and have explained much regarding mainstream Freemasonry and the more lesser known but equally as important rituals, there is so much more that I could have detailed, but in one book what I have included is enough. There are many more opportunities for further study and these are generally available within a well run study group.

Being a Masonic Researcher and Lecturer for over 3o years I feel that it is my responsibility to gain as much knowledge as possible . Hence my investigations have taken me to many places where I have obtained much knowledge that has greatly assisted in explaining particular aspects of the Craft and The Holy Royal Arch, and are fully explained in my books "SO YOU THINK YOU KNOW ABOUT FREEMASONRY" and "SO YOU THINK YOU KNOW ABOUT THE CHAPTER". The reading room of the British Library, Grand Lodge Library, being Deputy Librarian General for the S.R.I.A. and working in the H.Q. at Hampstead once a week for a couple of years, 3 visits to Rosslyn Chapel, time at the Library at Greenwich Observatory when it was open to the public, the many books I have acquired within my own library, many ancient rituals I have collected on my travels and investigations, all these elements have contributed greatly to the production of this book, which I trust enables Freemasons to select their path carefully within this wonderful fraternity in order to get as much of the right information that proves conducive to their total enjoyment within this PROGRESSIVE SOCIETY.

In writing this extensive detail regarding the many orders included in this Progressive Science, I sent to the Heads of the Orders within my own Province an exact copy of what I intended to commit to print concerning their particular Order. Not necessarily to obtain their permission, as we enjoy a society of free expression, but out of respect to let them know precisely what I was writing and to afford them the opportunity of adding any comments they wished to make. The majority replied with their agreement and some added some comments of their own which I, of course included. Very few failed to even reply, maybe only a couple.

Where I have specifically quoted from an actual book I have noted the accreditation accordingly. In the instance that I have extracted information from the internet I have duly acknowledged that extraction. Should there be any that I have forgotten then I apologise accordingly, as I am only human and by that fact am subject to error. Otherwise where it is not noted all the writing is my own from my knowledge and experience.

Thank you for your indulgence.
Ray Hudson, March 2020.

MASTER MASON

MASONIC ORDER OF THE GARTER

ROYAL ORDER OF ZANZIBAR

CORKS

ROYAL ARK MARINERS

MARK

CORPORATION O' SQUAREMEN

MEMBER OF MARK AND HRA

THE OPERATIVES

ROYAL AND SELECT MASTERS

PAST TIM AND INVITE ONLY

ORDER OF THE SILVER TROWEL

ALLIED MASONIC DEGREES

4 WEEKS A MASTER MASON

HOLY ROYAL ARCH

INVITATION ONLY

MEMBERSHIP OF ALLIED NOT A REQUIREMENT IN THE UK

THE HEROIC ORDER OF THE GORDIAN KNOT

KNIGHT MASONS

MASONIC ORDER OF ST. PATRICK

ANCIENT ORDER OF JONAH

ORDER OF THE SECRET MONITOR

ROYAL ORDER OF THE MASONIC KNIGHTS OF THE SCARLET CORD

20 MINUTE PAPER MUST BE SUBMITTED ON ANY ESOTERIC SUBJECT EXCEPT FREEMASONRY: ONLY ONE CHANCE IS GIVEN.

AUGUST ORDER OF LIGHT

BELIEF IN THE PRINCIPLES OF THE TRINITARIAN CHRISTIAN FAITH

RED CROSS OF CONSTANTINE

MASTER MASON FOR ONE YEAR

ANCIENT AND ACCEPTED RITE

SOCIETAS ROSICRUCIANA IN ANGLIA

MINIMUM ADEPTUS EXEMPTUS STRICT INVITATION ONLY

E.R.

INVITATION ONLY

MASONIC ORDER OF ATHELSTAN

KNIGHTS TEMPLAR

KNIGHTS OF MALTA

VARIOUS ENTRY REQUIREMENTS

KBHC (CBCS)

PAST FIRST PRINCIPLE HOLY ROYAL ARCH

PILGRIM PRECEPTORS

INSTALLED MASTER (CRAFT)

COMMEMORATIVE ORDER OF ST. THOMAS OF ACON

HOLY ROYAL ARCH KNIGHT TEMPLAR PRIESTS

MASTER MASON FOR 5 YEARS PLUS VARIOUS OTHER REQUIREMENTS DEPENDING ON PROVINCE: TYPICALLY SENIOR KT AND OR ABAR

ROYAL ORDER OF SCOTLAND

BY STRICT INVITATION ONLY

ZELATOR

HERMETIC ORDER OF MARTINISTS

BY STRICT INVITATION ONLY

ROSE CROIX 67 ORIENT

ELUS COHEN

SWEDENBORG RITE

ORDER OF PALERMO (THE ILLUMINATI)

ANCIENT AND ILLUSTRIOUS ORDER OF KNIGHT MALTA

HERMETIC CHAPTER OF THE SPIRITUAL KNIGHT

INVITATION ONLY

MEMPHIS MISRAIM

FELLOWSHIP OF THE ROSE CROSS

CELTIC CROSS

ORDER OF THE GRASSHOPPER

ORDER OF THE GOLDEN CENTURE

THE OLD MAN OF THE MOUNTAIN (THE GRAND ORIENT OF ALAMUT)

ORDER OF ELIAS THE ARTIST

ORDER OF HERMES TRISMEGISTUS

KNIGHTS OF THE HOLY GRAIL

KNIGHTS OF THE PARACLETE

ANCIENT ESSENIAC ORDERS

MASONIC DRUIDS

ROSICRUCIAN ORDER OF THE GRAIL

ROSICRUCIANA ANTIQUA

FRATERNITY ROSICRUCENSIS

TEMPLAR FRATERNITY OF MIRRIAM

ORDER OF THE FIFTH EMPIRE

AZILOTH ||| BOOKS

Aziloth Books publishes a wide range of titles ranging from hard-to-find esoteric books - *Parchment Books* - to classic works on fiction, politics and philosophy - *Cathedral Classics*. Our newest venture is *Aziloth Books Children's Classics*, with vibrant new covers and illustrations to complement some of the world's very best children's tales. All our imprints are offered to the reader at a competitive price and through as many mediums and outlets as possible.

We are committed to excellent book production and strive, whenever possible, to add value to our titles with original images, maps and author introductions. With the premium on space in most modern dwellings, we also endeavour - within the limits of good book design - to make our products as slender as possible, allowing more books to be fitted into a given bookshelf area.

We are a small, approachable company and would love to hear any of your comments and suggestions on our plans, products, or indeed on absolutely anything.

Aziloth Books, Rimey Law, Rookhope, Co. Durham, DL13 2BL, England.
t: 01388-517600 e: info@azilothbooks.com w: www.azilothbooks.com

PARCHMENT BOOKS enshrines the concept of the oneness of all true religious traditions - that "the light shines from many different lanterns". Our list below offers titles from both eastern and western spiritual traditions, including Christian, Judaic, Islamic, Daoist, Hindu and Buddhist mystical texts, as well as books on alchemy, hermeticism, paganism, etc..

By bringing together such spiritual texts, we hope to make esoteric and occult knowledge more readily available to those ready to receive it. We do not publish grimoires or titles pertaining to the left hand path. Titles include:

The Prophet; The Madman: Parables & Poems	Khalil Gibran
Abandonment to Divine Providence	Jean-Pierre de Caussade
Corpus Hermeticum	G. R. S. Mead (trans.)
The Holy Rule of St Benedict	St. Benedict of Nursia
The Confession of St Patrick	St. Patrick
The Outline of Sanity	G. K. Chesterton
An Outline of Occult Science	Rudolf Steiner
The Dialogue Of St Catherine Of Siena	St. Catherine of Siena
Esoteric Christianity; Thought-Forms*	Annie Besant
The Teachings of Zoroaster	Shapurji A. Kapadia
Daemonologie	King James of England
A Dweller on Two Planets	Phylos the Thibetan
Bushido*	Nitobe Inazo
The Interior Castle	St. Teresa of Avila
Songs of Innocence & Experience*	William Blake
The Secret of the Rosary	St. Louis Marie de Montfort
From Ritual to Romance	Jessie L. Weston
The God of the Witches	Margaret Murray
Kundalini – an occult experience	George S. Arundale
The Kingdom of God is Within You	Leo Tolstoy
The Trial and Death of Socrates	Plato
A Textbook of Theosophy	Charles W. Leadbetter
Chuang Tzu: Daoist Teachings	Chuang Tzu
Practical Mysticism	Evelyn Underhill
Tao Te Ching (Lao Tzu's 'Book of the Way')	Tzu, Lao
The Most Holy Trinosophia	Le Comte de St.-Germain
Tertium Organum	P. D. Ouspensky
Totem and Taboo	Sigmund Freud
The Kebra Negast	E. A. Wallis Budge
Esoteric Buddhism	Alfred Percy Sinnett
Demian: the story of a youth	Hermann Hesse

* with colour illustrations

Obtainable at all good online and local bookstores.
View Aziloth Books' full list at: www.azilothbooks.com

CATHEDRAL CLASSICS hosts an array of classic literature, from erudite ancient tomes to avant-garde, twentieth-century masterpieces, all of which deserve a place in your home. All the world's great novelists are here, Jane Austen, Dickens, Conrad, Arthur Machen and Henry James, brushing shoulders with such disparate luminaries as Sun Tzu, Marcus Aurelius, Kipling, Friedrich Nietzsche, Machiavelli, and Omar Khayam. A small selection is detailed below:

Frankenstein	Mary Shelley
Herland; With Her in Ourland	Charlotte Perkins Gilman
The Time Machine; The Invisible Man	H. G. Wells
Three Men in a Boat	Jerome K Jerome
The Rubaiyat of Omar Khayyam	Omar Khayyam
A Study in Scarlet; The Sign of the Four	Arthur Conan Doyle
The Picture of Dorian Gray	Oscar Wilde
Flatland	Edwin A. Abbott
The Coming Race	Bulwer Lytton
The Adventures of Sherlock Holmes	Arthur Conan Doyle
The Great God Pan	Arthur Machen
Beyond Good and Evil	Friedrich Nietzsche
England, My England	D. H. Lawrence
The Castle of Otranto	Horace Walpole
Self-Reliance, & Other Essays (series1&2)	Ralph W. Emmerson
The Art of War	Sun Tzu
A Shepherd's Life	W. H. Hudson
The Double	Fyodor Dostoyevsky
To the Lighthouse; Mrs Dalloway	Virginia Woolf
Leaves of Grass - 1855 edition	Walt Whitman
Analects	Confucius
Beowulf	Anonymous
The Subjection of Women	John Stuart Mill
The Rights of Man	Thomas Paine
Progress and Poverty	Henry George
Captain Blood	Rafael Sabatini
Captains Courageous	Rudyard Kipling
The Meditations of Marcus Aurelius	Marcus Aureliu
The Social Contract	Jean Jacques Rousseau
War is a Racket	Smedley D. Butler
The Dead	James Joyce
The Old Wives' Tale	Arnold Bennett

Obtainable at all good online and local bookstores.
View Aziloth Books' full list at: www.azilothbooks.com

AZILOTH BOOKS | CHILDREN'S Classics

Aziloth Books is passionate about bringing the very best in children's classics fiction to the next generation of book-lovers. We believe in the transforming power of children's books to encourage a life-long love of reading, and publish only the best authors and illustrators. With its original design and outstanding quality, our highly successful list has something to suit every age and interest. Titles include:

The Railway Children	Edith Nesbit
Anne of Green Gables	Lucy Maud Montgomery
What Katy Did	Susan Coolidge
Puck of Pook's Hill	Rudyard Kipling
The Jungle Books	Rudyard Kipling
Just So Stories	Rudyard Kipling
Alice Through the Looking Glass	Charles Dodgson
Alice's Adventures in Wonderland*	Charles Dodgson
Black Beauty	Anna Sewell
The War of the Worlds	H. G Wells
The Time Machine	H. G .Wells
The Sleeper Awakes	H. G. Wells
The Invisible Man	H. G. Wells
The Lost World	Sir Arthur Conan Doyle
Gulliver's Travels*	Jonathan Swift
Catriona (David Balfour)	Robert Louis Stevenson
The Water Babies	Charles Kingsley
The First Men in the Moon	Jules Verne
The Secret Garden	Frances Hodgson Burnett
A Little Princess	Frances Hodgson Burnett
Peter Pan*	J. M. Barrie
The Song of Hiawatha*	Henry W. Longfellow
Tales from Shakespeare	Charles & Mary Lamb
The Wonderful Wizard of Oz	L. Frank Baum

*with colour illustrations

Obtainable at all good online and local bookstores.
View Aziloth Books' full list at: www.azilothbooks.com

www.ingramcontent.com/pod-product-compliance
Lightning Source LLC
Chambersburg PA
CBHW050843270326
41930CB00019B/3451